**EVANSTON · PUBLIC
LIBRARY**

*Purchase of this library
material made possible
by a contribution
to the Fund for Excellence*

_____

_____

_____

_____

American Habitats

Wetland Animals

Connor Dayton

PowerKiDS press.

New York

Published in 2009 by The Rosen Publishing Group, Inc.
29 East 21st Street, New York, NY 10010

First Edition

Editor: Nicole Pristash
Book Design: Greg Tucker
Photo Researcher: Jessica Gerweck

Photo Credits: Cover, back cover, pp. 7, 9, 13, 15, 17 Shutterstock.com; p. 5 © Norbert Rosing/Getty Images; p. 11 © Shin Yoshino/Getty Images; p. 19 © Eduardo Velasco/Getty Images; p. 21 © Tim Fitzharris/Getty Images.

Library of Congress Cataloging-in-Publication Data

Dayton, Connor.
  Wetland animals / Connor Dayton. — 1st ed.
      p. cm. — (American habitats)
  Includes index.
  ISBN 978-1-4358-2769-1 (library binding) — ISBN 978-1-4358-3198-8 (pbk.)
ISBN 978-1-4358-3204-6 (6-pack)
  1. Wetland animals—Juvenile literature. I. Title.
  QL113.8.D39 2009
  591.768—dc22

                          2008039704

Manufactured in the United States of America

Contents

America's Wetland Animals

A wetland is a **habitat** in which low-lying land meets water. The land in a wetland habitat is generally wet and muddy. Wetlands can be found all over the world, and many can be found in the United States.

A wetland is an important part of our world. It is home to lots of animals. If you visit a wetland, you can see mallard ducks swimming in the water, frogs jumping from place to place, and dragonflies flying through the air. Put on your rubber boots and get ready to learn more about the animals that live in America's wetlands!

These river otters are keeping watch in some grass. River otters are just some of the animals that live in America's wetland habitats.

Wet Ground

A wetland is land that is **saturated** with water. It is an interesting place. A wetland is not wet enough to be considered a pond or a lake, but it is too wet to be considered dry land. In a wetland habitat, you can find animals living on the drier parts of the wetland and in the water as well.

Frogs and toads get to live in both parts of a wetland because they are amphibians. Amphibians are animals that spend the early parts of their lives in the water and the rest of their lives on land!

Shown here is part of the Everglades, in southern Florida. The Everglades is one of the largest wetlands in the United States.

A Wetland Is a Home

A wetland habitat is rich with plant life, so it is a good place for plant-eating animals to live. Marshes, for example, are **shallow** wetlands that have rich soil. Plants, such as **reeds** and **cattails**, grow in big numbers there. These plants are food for some wetland animals. The plants are also good places for wetland animals, such as birds and muskrats, to make their homes.

Muskrats are medium-sized **mammals** that look like big rats. Muskrats are great swimmers. They can often be spotted diving into the marsh water to eat plants and small fish.

This muskrat is sitting on some thin ice in a wetland. A muskrat's fur allows the muskrat to go into icy water to find underwater plants to eat.

A Place to Work and Play

The beaver is another mammal that lives in America's wetlands. Beavers build cone-shaped homes, called lodges. First, the beavers use their sharp teeth to cut up sticks and branches. Then, the beavers build the lodge with the sticks, branches, and some mud. These lodges are built strong so that other animals cannot get in them.

River otters are mammals that spend most of their lives in the water. When they are not hunting for fish and frogs to eat, otters play. You might see river otters using a muddy riverbank as a slide!

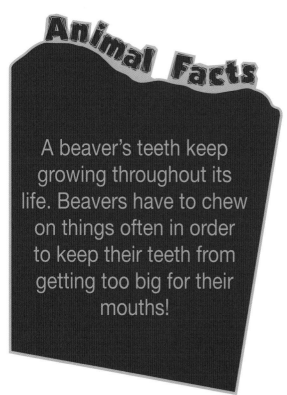

Animal Facts

A beaver's teeth keep growing throughout its life. Beavers have to chew on things often in order to keep their teeth from getting too big for their mouths!

Here you can see a beaver swimming with a tree branch in its mouth. The beaver will use this branch to build a lodge.

Ducks on the Water

If you have been to a wetland, you have likely seen birds. The mallard duck is one of the most common birds in America's wetlands. The male mallard has a bright green head, a gray body, and a yellow bill. Male mallard ducks are called drakes. The female mallard duck is light brown in color, and it has a dark brown bill.

Mallards build nests near the water. They spend their days floating along the water looking for fish, amphibians, and water plants to eat. Sometimes, you can see them dunking their heads under water to get these foods!

This mother mallard duck is swimming through a wetland with her babies.
Baby ducks are called ducklings.

Great Blue Herons

Great blue herons are grayish blue, long-legged birds that live in wetlands throughout the United States. They are the biggest and most common herons in America. Great blue herons build nests in trees high above the wetland in groups, called colonies.

A great blue heron's main food is fish. When a heron hunts, it walks slowly through the water and waits for a fish to swim by. When that happens, the great blue heron wounds the fish with its long bill and then swallows the fish whole! Great blue herons also eat mice and **insects**.

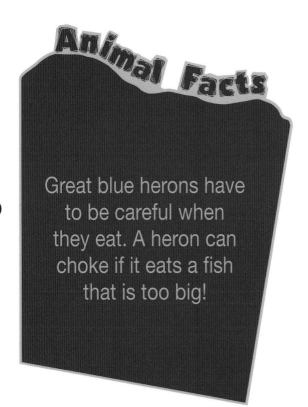

Animal Facts

Great blue herons have to be careful when they eat. A heron can choke if it eats a fish that is too big!

Here two great blue herons are shown standing in their nest. A great blue heron's nest is made of sticks, moss, plants, and dry grass.

Many types of insects can be spotted darting around a wetland habitat. Dragonflies are often seen the most. Dragonflies have thin bodies, and they are very fast fliers. Their long wings help them fly. A dragonfly's colorful wings measure around 6 inches (15 cm) from one wing tip to the other wing tip.

Dragonflies have large eyes that allow them to see what is around them. Having good eyesight allows dragonflies to not only hunt for food, but also to fly away from the birds, frogs, and fish that like to eat them!

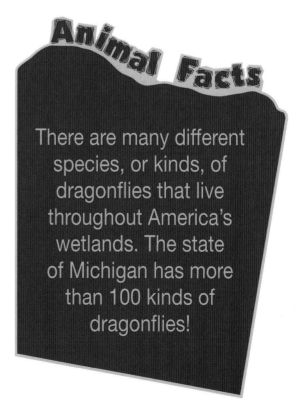

Animal Facts

There are many different species, or kinds, of dragonflies that live throughout America's wetlands. The state of Michigan has more than 100 kinds of dragonflies!

Dragonflies, like the one shown here, do not bite people. Dragonflies feed on insects, such as mosquitoes, spiders, and even other dragonflies.

In the Water

Because a wetland has so much water, it is only natural that many fish and underwater animals live there. The salt marshes along the East Coast are full of fish. Flounder, for example, go to salt marshes to **mate**. The baby fish live in the marsh until they are big enough to move out to the ocean.

The blue crab, another wetland water animal, is named for its blue claws. This **crustacean** lives in the salt marshes around Maryland's Chesapeake Bay. It feeds along the bottom of the marsh, eating plants, clams, and other blue crabs!

Blue crabs, like this one, use their powerful claws to gather food, to dig in sand, and to keep themselves safe.

Amphibians

The lives of amphibians, such as frogs and toads, are all about water. When they are born, frogs and toads are called tadpoles. Tadpoles swim around and breathe underwater, as fish do. As tadpoles get older, they lose their tails. Next, tadpoles grow legs and lungs that breathe air. When frogs and toads are grown, they live on land. However, they stay near water because they need to keep their skin from drying out.

Northern leopard frogs can be found near marshes throughout the United States. Leopard frogs have dark spots on their bodies, as leopards do.

The northern leopard frog, shown here, is 3 to 5 inches (8–13 cm) long. This frog generally lives two to four years in the wild.

Conserving Wetlands

Mammals, birds, insects, and many other animals live in America's wetlands, but wetlands are becoming **endangered**. Wetlands are often changed so that buildings can be built on them. Some wetlands have become **polluted**, too. These things take the wetland habitat away from the animals that live there. Some wetland animals have nearly died out.

People, though, are working to **conserve** wetlands and the animals that live in them. Perhaps you can help by getting your community to work together to clean up marshes and wetlands where you live. Doing so can keep the wetland habitat alive for a long time!

endangered (in-DAYN-jerd) In danger of no longer existing.

habitat (HA-beh-tat) The kind of land where animals or plants naturally live.

insects (IN-sekts) Small animals that often have six legs and wings.

mammals (MA-mulz) Animals that have a backbone and feed milk to their young.

mate (MAYT) To come together to make babies.

polluted (puh-LOO-ted) Hurt by unsafe matter.

reeds (REEDZ) Tall, thin grasses.

saturated (SA-chur-ayt-ed) Completely filled with something, such as water.

shallow (SHA-loh) Not deep.

Index

Web Sites

Due to the changing nature of Internet links, PowerKids Press has developed an online list of Web sites related to the subject of this book. This site is updated regularly. Please use this link to access the list:

www.powerkidslinks.com/amhab/wetland/